COMMUNITY · CONNECTIONS

WHAT'S IT LIKE TO LIVE HERE?
MINING TOWN

BY KATIE MARSICO

Published in the United States of America by Cherry Lake Publishing
Ann Arbor, Michigan
www.cherrylakepublishing.com

Content Adviser: James Wolfinger, PhD, Associate Professor of History,
DePaul University, Chicago, Illinois
Reading Adviser: Marla Conn, ReadAbility, Inc.

Photo Credits: Cover and page 1, ©Jeff Morgan 03/Alamy; page 5, ©wandee007/
Shutterstock, Inc.; page 7, ©Jiri Vaclavek/Shutterstock, Inc.; page 9, ©matthi/Shutterstock, Inc.;
page 11, ©Jacek Chabraszewski/Shutterstock, Inc.; page 13, ©Monkey Business Images/
Shutterstock, Inc.; page 15, ©huyangshu/Shutterstock, Inc.; page 17, ©kuznetcov_konstantin/
Shutterstock, Inc.; page 19, USFS Region 5 / http://www.flickr.com / CC BY 2.0; page 21,
©kolessl/Shutterstock, Inc.

LIBRARY OF CONGRESS CATALOGING-IN-PUBLICATION DATA
Marsico, Katie, 1980– What's It Like to Live Here?:
  Mining town / by Katie Marsico.
      pages cm. — (Community connections)
  Includes bibliographical references and index.
  ISBN 978-1-62431-566-4 (lib. bdg.) — ISBN 978-1-62431-590-9 (ebook) —
ISBN 978-1-62431-582-4 (pbk.) — ISBN 978-1-62431-574-9 (pdf)
  1. Mining camps—Juvenile literature. 2. Mines and mineral resources—Juvenile literature.
I. Title.
  TN148.M28 2013
  307.76'6—dc23   2013028551

Cherry Lake Publishing would like to acknowledge the
work of The Partnership for 21st Century Skills. Please
visit www.p21.org for more information.

Printed in the United States of America
Corporate Graphics Inc.
January 2014

CONTENTS

BOOM!

Sam was enjoying an afternoon picnic in the park. Tall gray-brown hills towered in the distance. The park was fairly quiet until . . . boom! Sam heard a blast far away across the hilltops. He wasn't startled, though. These blasts were common in mining towns like the one Sam lived in.

Mine blasts that occur at ground level can be especially loud!

Why would loud booms be common in a mining town? Miners often blow up rocks to break them apart. It makes it easier to collect ore. This process is known as blasting. The boom it creates is a common sound in mining towns.

5

Mining towns are home mainly to miners and their families. Miners collect **minerals** and other materials from the earth. Examples of minerals are coal, gold, iron, and copper. Miners work in mines and **quarries**. The towns where they live are built nearby. These **communities** help shape the **culture** and **economy** of entire countries.

Some miners collect gemstones such as amethyst.

Can you guess how long mining towns have existed? These communities date back hundreds of years. However, communities change. When mines close, nearby residents usually leave. Such mining towns are often called ghost towns.

7

OFF TO SCHOOL

Sam woke early the next day. His dad already had breakfast ready. Sam's mom had left for work before Sam woke up. She would work 12 hours in the nearby mine. It was the first day of her **shift**. She would have a few days off in a week. Sam rarely saw her during her shift.

Many miners work long days, just like Sam's mom.

Do you know any kids who live in mining towns? Ask them about their parents' jobs. When do the parents go to work and come home? Do they work on weekends? Are they away for long stretches of time? Do the kids have to do extra chores to help out at home?

9

Sam grabbed his bag and his bike. His friend Jess was outside. Her little sister was with her. The three of them biked to school together each morning. They took a short cut through the woods. Sam always liked the short cut. It was one of the best things about living in a **remote** area.

Residents of mining towns often live near scenic natural areas.

LOOK!

Look up photos of modern mining towns. Find pictures that show the natural areas around these communities. Many remote mining towns are close to wilderness. Rivers, hills, canyons, and forests are often found there.

INTO THE MINE

Sam was excited when he arrived at school. This was the day his class visited the mine. Nearly all of his friends had parents who worked there. Plus, Sam loved geology. This is the study of the earth's rocks. A mine is a perfect place to learn about that!

Most of the kids in Sam's class had parents who worked at the mine.

LOOK!

Go on the Internet or visit the library. Find photos of modern mining towns. One example is Wabush, Newfoundland and Labrador. You can also look up Superior, Arizona. What buildings do you see in these communities? Can you find pictures of local mines?

13

Sam's class rode a school bus to the mine. There, people worked big machines. Trucks drove in and out of the area. Everyone wore bright vests and hardhats. The bus stopped and Sam's class got out. A man handed everyone vests and hardhats of their own. He explained that they had to wear them for safety.

Miners use bulldozers and other machinery to collect minerals.

ASK QUESTIONS!

Talk to people living in a mining town. Have they ever seen mining machinery in their community? Do they know what it is used for? Some machinery can be dangerous. Do residents have to follow special rules to stay safe?

The man's name was Mr. Daniels. He took the students into parts of the mine. There, they saw some of the machines work. Mr. Daniels talked about what different workers did. He also talked about coal. This is the mineral found in the mine. Coal is a fuel. It is burned to create electricity.

It is not unusual for mines to operate all day, every day.

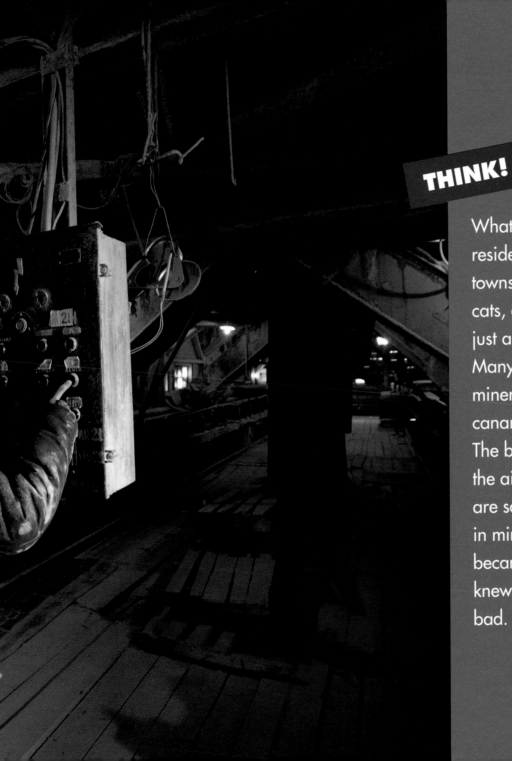

THINK!

What kinds of pets do residents of mining towns own? Dogs, cats, and fish are just a few examples! Many years ago, miners brought canaries to work. The birds helped test the air. Deadly gases are sometimes found in mines. If the birds became sick, miners knew the air was bad.

CELEBRATING

The town held a mining festival that evening. Sam went with his dad and brother after school. Many of Sam's neighbors were there. There were also visitors from out of town. They came to celebrate the community. They also came to learn more about the mine.

Festivals give both locals and visitors a chance to celebrate and learn about mining.

MAKE A GUESS!

Can you guess how many people live in mining towns? It depends on the town! In 2011, Wabush, Canada, had fewer than 2,000 residents. Superior, Arizona, was home to about 3,000 people.

19

Sam realized how important the mine was. Most of the adults he knew depended on it for jobs. What if the mine closed down? Families would have to move away to find work. Mining was a hard job. Sam often missed his mom. But his whole family worked together for one another and the community.

Families in mining towns often try to work together as a team. They help support one another and their community.

CREATE!

Use clay to create a model of a mining town. Show homes, stores, and natural areas that border the community. Remember to add clay sculptures of local mining operations as well. Look at pictures of Wabush, Superior, and other mining towns for ideas of what else to include in your model.

21

GLOSSARY

communities (kuh-MYOO-nut-eez) places and the people who live in them

culture (KUHL-chur) the ideas, customs, traditions, and way of life of a group of people

economy (i-KAH-nuh-mee) a system of buying, selling, making things, and managing money

minerals (MIN-uh-ruhlz) solid substances found in the earth that do not come from an animal or plant

ore (OR) a rock that contains a metal or valuable mineral

quarries (KWOR-eez) places where stone, slate, or sand is dug from the ground

remote (ri-MOHT) far away, secluded, or isolated

residents (REZ-uh-dents) people who live in a particular place on a long-term basis

shift (SHIFT) time period during which someone is at work

FIND OUT MORE

BOOKS

Gordon, Nick. *Coal Miner.* Minneapolis: Bellwether Media, 2013.

Hyde, Natalie. *Life in a Mining Community.* New York: Crabtree Publishing, 2010.

Tieck, Sarah. *Miners.* Edina, MN: ABDO Publishing, 2012.

WEB SITES

The William E. Hewit Institute—Miners of Colorado
http://hewit.unco.edu/dohist/teachers/essays/miners.htm
Review this site for a description of a 19th-century Colorado mining town, including details that explain what life was like for local children.

United States Department of Labor—Mine Safety and Health Administration's Kids' Page
www.msha.gov/kids/kidshp.htm
Check out this page for more information on mining, including safety tips and historical data.

INDEX

ABOUT THE AUTHOR

Katie Marsico is the author of more than 100 children's books. She lives in a suburb of Chicago, Illinois, with her husband and children.